Word Bird™

Makes Words
With Cat

Published in the United States of America by The Child's World®, Inc.
PO Box 326
Chanhassen, MN 55317-0326
800-599-READ
www.childsworld.com

Project Manager Mary Berendes
Editor Katherine Stevenson, Ph.D.
Designer Ian Butterworth

Library of Congress Cataloging-in-Publication Data
Moncure, Jane Belk.
Word Bird makes words with Cat : a short "a" adventure / by Jane Belk Moncure.
p. cm.
Summary: When his father brings home new word puzzles,
Word Bird makes up words with his friend Cat,
and each new word leads them into a new activity.
ISBN 1-56766-899-2 (lib. bdg.)
[1. Vocabulary. 2. Birds—Fiction. 3. Cats—Fiction.] I. Title.
PZ7.M739 Wnce 2001
[E]—dc21
00-010892

Word  Bird™

Makes Words With Cat

by Jane Belk Moncure

illustrated by Chris McEwan

"What is in the box?" asked
Word Bird one day.

WORD
PUZZLES
Short a

"Word puzzles," said Papa.

"I can put word puzzles together. I can make words," said Word Bird.

Word Bird put

c with at.

What did Word Bird make?

c at

Just then, Cat came to play.

"I can make words, too,"
said Cat.

Cat put

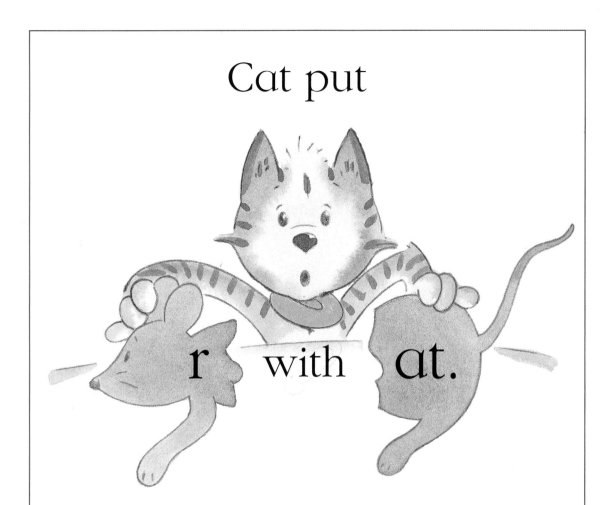

r with at.

What word did Cat make?

r at

Then Word Bird put

h with at.

What did Word Bird make?

"Let's play with hats,"
said Cat. And they did.

Then Word Bird put

v with an.

What did Word Bird make?

v an

Cat put

p with an.

What word did Cat make?

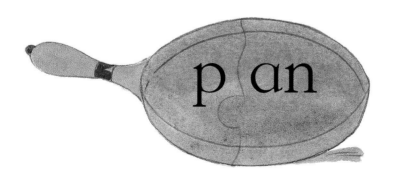

p an

Word Bird put

f with an.

What did Word Bird make?

f an

"I'm hot," said Cat.
"Let's turn on the fan."

Word Bird put

b with ag.

What did Word Bird make?

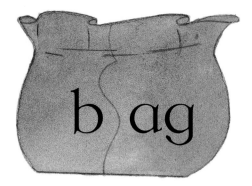

b ag

Cat put

fl with ag.

What word did Cat make?

fl ag

...into the kitchen.
Mama gave them apples
for a snack.

Cat put

fl with ag.

What word did Cat make?

fl ag

"Let's make flags and march," said Word Bird.

They marched and
marched…

...into the kitchen.
Mama gave them apples
for a snack.

"Let's make more words," said Word Bird.

Word Bird put

c with ab.

What did Word Bird make?

c ab

"Let's go to the sandbox in my cab," said Word Bird.

"Let's play in the sand," said Cat. So they did.

They made roads...lots of
sand roads.

They made hills…lots of sand hills.

They made a
sand castle, too.

Word Bird was happy
because Cat did not
throw sand.

Cat sat and played like a good cat.

Then Mama said, "Come here, Word Bird. I have a puzzle for you."

Mama put

n with ap.

What did Mama make?

Word Bird did not
read the word.

Word Bird was already
taking a nap.

You can read more word
puzzles with Word Bird.

f at

p at

r ag

t ag

c ap

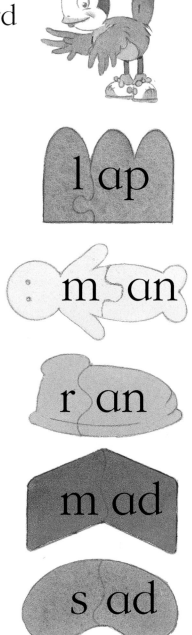

l ap

m an

r an

m ad

s ad

Now you can make some word puzzles.